A Grandchild's Guide to the Journey

REED MORRISON

LUMINARE PRESS

WWW.LUMINAREPRESS.COM

Printed in the United States of America

Illustrations by Olivia Bressler, BFA and Talia Morrison, LMFT

Author Photograph by David Mathai, MD

Luminare Press
442 Charnelton St.
Eugene, OR 97401
www.luminarepress.com

LCCN: 2023908797
ISBN: 979-8-88679-286-7

We are all grandchildren.

TABLE OF CONTENTS

Two Fools 1

Two Worlds 6

What's Inside? 24

Warmer-Colder 31

When Warm is Hot 40

Character 46

Failure 50

Synchronicity 53

Dreams! 59

Nightmares! 64

Waking Nightmares? 69

Loneliness 72

Meditation 77

Your Turn 86

Acknowledgements 88

TWO FOOLS

Allow me to introduce myself.

I am an old voice for you to carry with you, I am DNA that you already carry and I am a guide for travels that lie ahead.

Please forgive me for not writing sooner, but a book like this can only be written in the last part of a life.

You see, a climb up a mountain takes a long time, but the effort is well worth it, if only for the view.

Ah, the view! From here I can see the whole of my life, the routes I've taken, the wrong turns and dead-ends, the lucky short-cuts and the paths of others that crossed my own.

But why listen to an old person? Aren't old people called "old fools"? And who wants to listen to a fool?

But wait, there are young fools too!

In fact, the real meaning of "fool", according to scholars of myths and legends, is a young person who is beginning a life journey. It's someone who is not yet sure of who they are, what they should do and what they should not do, but at the same time curious and determined to learn about themselves and the world.

The fool is a seeker of experience, knowledge and wisdom.

And so, the young fool embarks on a life journey and gathers a lifetime of experiences and wisdom until, in old age, they hand-off what they learned to someone who is young.

It's a gift that must be made for the old one's journey to be complete and for the young one's journey to begin.

This Guide is my gift to you.

TWO WORLDS

We have a lot in common, you and I. Both seekers, young and old. Both journeyers on our paths.

I have been where you are, so in some ways I am you.

And we could say that you are me, but in a younger body and in a different time and place.

Although we live in different times, we also live in the same places.

In the same kinds of worlds.

Let me explain.

The word "world" is used in lots of ways, usually to describe our planet or a map of all the places on our planet. I'm going to use it in another way.

I will use it to mean the place of our experience. Not just a physical place, but a feeling-experience of place.

You know this intuitively.

Intuition, by the way, is a way of knowing without knowing how you know. You just know it, in a very mysterious, affirming, special-feeling kind of way. In your bones. We'll be talking more about intuition as we travel on.

Let's get started.

First, the two of us, and everyone else, live in two worlds.

By this I don't mean two cities or neighborhoods, schools, houses or families. I mean in two different worlds of experience.

Each of us, no matter who we are, experiences an outside and an inside to life.

Again, you intuitively know this.

We can call the outside of life the Outer World and the inside of life the Inner World.

Each of us lives in both of them.

Both at the same time.

I'll try to explain.

Let's start with the Outer World.

The Outer World is the one we hear, feel, taste, touch and smell. We can measure it and move in it. It has dimensions and weight. It's the place of science, the place where we meet our families, our friends and everything and everyone we love.

We create in this world and succeed and sometimes fail in this world.

It's the stage upon which we play our lives.

The Outer World also goes by other names, like "Objective World" and "Real World".

The Inner World is invisible to our "outer eyes" and outer senses. But it is no less real than the one we call the Outer World.

The Inner World is where we dream, imagine, where we have private thoughts, prayers, conversations with ourselves and fantasies of all kinds.

It's where we feel hope and happiness and it's where we also feel fear, sadness and sometimes hopelessness.

The Inner World is a private place where we talk and argue with ourselves, cry with ourselves and celebrate with ourselves.

It's where creativity is born and lives and where it can some-times seem to disappear.

It's the place of imagination.

What's most important is that the Inner World is where we experience our knowing and feeling of self.

It's the world where we feel ourselves as an "I", an "I" that's a "me"!

The Inner World also has other names, like the "Subjective World" and the "Phenomenal World".

The seeable and touchable Outer World is visible and constantly changes.

You know this.

Sometimes we can barely keep up with the changes in technology, places, friends, how we speak, the music we make and hear and the art we make and see. The long list of changes in the Outer World gets longer by the day and sometimes by the minute.

What is new in the Outer World is constantly replacing what is old.

Although it's invisible to our eyes, the Inner World changes too.

But change is different in the Inner World.

It doesn't so much change as it grows. It grows in depths and textures that evolve over time. And, like vines and roots, it doesn't grow in straight lines. It finds its own way.

And sometimes it sprouts into new, unexpected shapes and forms.

Meanwhile, the seeds of your Inner World, that were planted when you were born, have sprouted and are growing.

Right now.

Like a young tree, your roots will strengthen and burrow deeper as your life moves ahead and your tree's leaves and branches will reach out in directions that will amaze, astound and some-times confound you.

Have I confused you?

Using the words "Inner" and "Outer" in these ways can create confusion. It makes it sound as if one exists inside our skins and the other outside our skins. Or that one is more real than the other.

This is not true, although we often think about them that way.

In truth, the two worlds are intertwined and connected.

They are both real and they are both us.

You see, these two worlds are connected by the same brain that makes something quite miraculous called consciousness.

To have consciousness is to have the experience of awareness of yourself and others, the aware-ness that makes it possible to think about and act on the fact that we are alive.

I wrote this Guide for many reasons. One is because I wish I had such a book when I was your age, but I didn't. Although, I did find guides along the way. I wish someone had told me about these two worlds when I was your age.

But no one told me.

I wish I had known there was such a thing as an Inner World and what we will come to call an Inner Life.

This Guide will have little to say about the Outer World except as it relates to our inner experience of it.

I am old and much about the outer world I inhabited has changed, but the Inner World, as I have experienced it, has not changed.

It can never be outdated.

This doesn't mean the Outer World is not important. It's very important, but it can't stand alone by itself very well. It needs the Inner World to give it strong roots and direction and meaning and completeness.

To give it life.

Knowing the Inner World helps to make sense of life as a living, connected whole.

I like to say that this Guide is about looking at life from the inside and living from the inside out.

WHAT'S INSIDE?

There is an Inner Life.

And even though it's invisible and mysterious, we can locate it.

Sort of...

It's in the place where the "you" that you feel is "you" is located.

The place of your "you-ness".

Clear? No?

Fair enough, I'll try to be more specific.

It's in the center of you.

Not the center of your body, although you may feel it in your heart.

I'm talking about the center of your being, the absolute center of your "you-ness".

We'll call this center the Self. Not the ordinary small "s" self of the body we see in the mirror, but the invisible, felt center of your Inner Life.

There are many, many names for the Self. Every language, every culture, every religion has at least one name for the Self, sometimes many. The words soul and psyche are ones we often hear and read about and ones I like very much.

But, to keep it simple for now, let's stick to Self.

Living from the inside out is using the Self as a guide.

Some imagine it as a compass.

A compass, if we know how to use it, shows us where we are in the physical world. If we get lost in the woods, a compass can show us a direction home.

It doesn't take us there, but it gives us a direction we can take. If we want to take it.

Like a compass, the Self, can give us directions.

It shows us where we can choose to go, but like a compass, it doesn't take us there.

When we feel lost in our lives, it can point to a new direction, but it doesn't do the work of taking us where we need to go.

That's up to us.

Remember, the fool becomes the wise person by making a journey through life.

The compass-like Self gives us the "trail markers", but we are the ones who must follow the trail.

The experiences we gain by losing our way, making choices and finding our way, create wisdom.

OK, so how do we use this inner Self compass? How do we know which direction the Self points? And where is it, exactly? These are important questions!

WARMER-COLDER

There are many ways to connect with the Self and we will explore some of them as we go on, but let's start with the first one I learned to use.

I still rely on it.

I call it "Warmer-Colder".

It's based on a game I remember from my childhood. Maybe you've played it too.

The Warmer-Colder game, as I remember it, went like this:

One player, the "hider", hides an object in a room and another player, who we can call the "seeker", has to find it.

This would be easy, except the seeker wears a blindfold!

The blindfolded seeker, with hands reaching out in front, carefully steps through the room in search of the hidden object.

The hider watches and gives hints to the seeker. If the seeker moves in the direction of the hidden object, the hider says "you're getting warmer!"

If the seeker moves farther away from the object, the hider says "you're getting colder!"

The hider continues to announce "you're getting warmer" or "you're getting colder" as the seeker moves through the room.

Finally, if the seeker keeps following messages of "warmer", the seeker finds the hidden object and wins the game.

Remember, the Self is something that is intuitively known. Intuition, you recall, is when you know something without knowing how or why you know it.

You just know it.

In your gut and in your bones.

Intuitive knowing feels true.

It feels warm.

Some paths in life feel warm, others feel cold.

The warmer ones are often choices and directions that are more helpful than the colder ones.

The warm ones, more often than not, direct us to kindness, empathy and justice.

These are the ones that are right for us. Even if they may not be right for other people.

The Self lets us know what is warm and what is cold. Then, it's up to us to follow.

Can we always trust the warmer direction?

The Self "knows" where we need to go, but it's not always where we want to go.

The Self does not always point us to the easy path. In fact, it rarely does.

Rather, it directs us to experiences we need.

In order to grow, to become strong, to become wise.

But what if the path is not clearly marked?

Sleep on it! I mean this literally. Hit the pause button!

Delay your decision-making at least until the following day, after a night of sleep.

Why?

Because our brains are very active during sleep. Scientists tell us that during sleep, memories are sorted-out and re-arranged. New brain cells are grown. Our brains create new pathways for processing information and coping with stresses.

Our problems can look, feel and think very differently in the morning!

WHEN WARM IS HOT

Using the decision compass becomes more difficult when our bodies enter the game.

Sexual feelings, in particular, can overwhelm us and make demands that can overpower decision making.

Warmer can get much hotter!

Sex isn't bad and sexual thoughts and fantasies do not make us bad. It's all natural and sex is necessary for keeping the human race going.

And...

Decisions about sex need a good amount of wisdom and maturity.

The problem is, sex jumps into our lives at an age when we have very little of either.

This means the chances of making our lives and the lives of our sexual partners very messy, complicated and painful can be pretty great.

Love-making can be confusing.

This does not usually happen if decisions about love-making actually include love.

When real love is in the picture, our own happiness depends upon the happiness of another person or persons.

This means a great deal of sensitivity and compassion for our partner is needed.

Compassion means we can feel another person's suffering.

Their suffering becomes our suffering.

Of course, unprotected sex runs the risk of creating a new life.

And what about our responsibility for the happiness of a new life? And compassion for any suffering that results?

Things work out when making love means making happiness for others and ourselves.

Non-consensual sex and selfish sex are not love-making.

CHARACTER

All this goes back to following the Self.

What happens when we do?

Every time we follow the Self, we grow in character.

Character is made by what we choose to do and how we do it. It's made up of the stuff of who we are as a person.

The kind of person we are.

A strong character grows by following the Self, so a person of strong character will usually be wise, compassionate and loving.

But how do we know if our character is growing strong?

R-E-S-P-E-C-T

As we follow warm signals from the Self and our character grows, our self-respect grows and respect from others grows.

Strong character feels good and right when our choices and actions are directed by the Self.

Others know character by how we act.

Character is the sum of our choices, made visible.

FAILURE

What if we fail to follow the Self? What if we go in the wrong direction? Make the wrong choice?

We are all human and we are all influenced by other people, other ideas, trends, physical urges, advertising, social media and peer pressure.

You name it.

Distractions from the Self are everywhere!

And we all make mistakes, lots of them.

The question is, do we learn from them?

For a successful life, mistakes are a necessity. Mistakes create unwanted and sometimes painful opportunities to learn and grow.

Nothing is lost if learning is gained because learning is the way wisdom is made.

We know we are becoming wise when we are making new mistakes and not repeating the old ones over and over.

SYNCHRONICITY

Another way the Self communicates is by something called synchronicity.

Synchronicity happens when coincidences have meaning. Intuitive meaning, a feeling of knowing that comes from the Self.

It's as if the Self says "This is important, pay attention!"

Coincidences are events that are random, they have no Outer World logical connection.

But synchronicities live in the Inner World.

A coincidence becomes a synchronicity when the connection feels warm and meaningful.

For example, you're thinking about a friend, Jane, who moved out of town. You haven't heard from her in many years. Just then, a truck passes with the name Jane's Plumbing Service printed on its door. Then, out the blue, your phone rings and it's Jane!

You don't know why or how it happened, but it feels important.

It's warm.

The Self says, "Pay attention, follow the warmth. There's something interesting and possibly important going on here!"

This is the Self "speaking" and when the Self speaks, it's usually a good thing to listen.

Synchronicity connects the Inner and Outer Worlds.

It connects them in mysterious and interesting ways.

And for only a brief moment, we are whole.

Our two Worlds become one.

And don't worry about interpreting a synchronicity.

Don't feel you have to decode it and find a hidden message.

The Self will take care of that, in due time.

Just pay attention and enjoy the pleasure and excitement of having a synchronicity on your journey.

The Self will do the rest

DREAMS!

Another mysterious way the Self speaks is through dreams. When we go to sleep and dream, it can feel like we're in another world or like we're in a movie or a play. Everything looks and feels very real. We can move or even fly, see places, meet people and become part of a story that can be very ordinary or quite strange.

The dream is real in the Inner World.

Scientists who study dreaming know what our dreaming brains are doing, but the dream itself, the story, the images and the experiences of dreaming remain Inner World mysteries.

Dreams, like synchronicities, come from the Inner World.

The word "unconscious", another word for hidden parts of the Inner World, is often used when talking about where dreams come from.

Dreams enter the Outer World when we wake-up and remember them.

And when they do, our two worlds are once again joined in mystery.

And, like synchronicities, dreams don't always make sense in the Outer World.

Important dreams grab attention and stay in awareness for hours, days, sometimes years.

Once again, don't worry about decoding and interpreting dreams. Let the inner intelligence of the Self guide you.

Follow them in your thoughts, listen, play with their stories and images. Paint them, dance them, sing them, write them.

Continue them by dreaming-them-on in your imagination.

Feel them in your body.

Watch for their images and themes appearing in Outer World life.

Do you sense warm messages to consider?

Their meanings are yours alone.

NIGHTMARES!

Some dreams are scary, even terrifying.

Nightmares!

They take us to places we don't want to be, scenes we don't want to see and feelings that frighten us.

Sometimes we do things in nightmares we would never do in waking Outer World life.

Shameful things.

But don't worry! Nightmares are normal. Everyone has them.

Everything in the Inner World has a purpose, even nightmares!

But sometimes the purpose is hidden.

One hidden purpose of nightmares is that they can provide protection and teaching.

They can help us become aware of situations to avoid or problems that need new solutions.

When we remember and think through a nightmare, we can become better prepared to solve problems, face our fears and create new and better ways to handle difficult challenges.

Nightmares can also show us parts of ourselves that need healing and changing.

These may be parts of ourselves that make us uncomfortable.

Parts of ourselves we may not like.

This kind of awareness can be a signal to examine ourselves, work on accepting ourselves or learn to make important changes in our lives.

Sometimes we're afraid night-mares will keep coming back.

And they can.

But when we work on them, meaning thinking about them and trying to learn their lessons, they can change for the better and eventually disappear entirely.

WAKING NIGHTMARES?

At times, our waking life journeys feel like nightmares.

Especially when bad things happen or when we've made choices that turn out to be the wrong ones.

This happens to us all.

When possible, we can treat our "waking nightmares" like we treat our dreaming ones: learn as much as we can from them.

Let their lessons protect and teach us.

Make the necessary changes, no matter how difficult and scary.

This may be easier said than done.

Sometimes the Self seems to be silent, but patience with the Self pays off.

Wait, listen, follow.

LONELINESS

During nightmarish times, we can feel very alone.

And it's easy to feel sorry for ourselves. We all do.

But nightmarish times can be opportunities to reach out to family and friends and let them know we need their help.

We can let them be closer to us.

They may not be able to fix things, but they can make sure we're not going through hard times alone.

This makes a great difference.

And helps us remember to reach-out to them when they need us.

The journey can sometimes be hard and lonely.

We must help one another!

Nightmarish times are like storms that blow through life. When we're in the middle of a powerful storm, everything seems dark, dangerous and hopeless.

Like it will never end.

But when the storm passes, the sun shines again.

Stormy times in life, though scary, can be amazingly important.

During these times, we learn lots about ourselves, our strengths and weaknesses, about the value of the family and friends around us and about what's truly important in life.

This is the view from the Inner World.

From the Self.

MEDITATION

You probably have heard something about meditation, or you
may even be practicing it.

There may literally be thousands
of ways to meditate.

Some are quite formal and
structured.

We often think of meditation as sitting cross-legged in silence, or chanting words in an exotic language. There are great religious traditions of the East and West that offer precise instructions for meditation.

You may find yourself, at some points in your life, reading about them and trying them out.

But meditation is not limited to traditional methods.

At its most basic, meditation is about paying attention.

Paying attention is possible when our focus is the present.

Our thoughts very naturally move to the past and what we think will be the future.

There's nothing wrong with this. Thinking about the past is useful for helping us learn from what we already experienced.

Thinking about the future helps prepare for obstacles and opportunities.

Interestingly, we spend very little time in the present.

By the present I mean a place-of-mind where we are temporarily free from the past and future.

Truly paying attention.

Most meditation practices are about helping us be in the present.

These are methods for quieting our thoughts and ridding ourselves of distractions from past and future.

Some of these methods use the breath, body movements and/or certain words spoken aloud or held in silence.

When our minds are quiet we can more easily observe our thoughts and we can weed-out unhelpful ones, including negative judgments we have about ourselves and others.

Sitting in stillness is only one way to enter a mind-place of meditation.

Others may involve movement, painting, writing, singing, hiking, making music, friendship, sports, helping people in need.

No matter how we get there, meditation is a way of being in the world where we are paying close attention to how we think, how we live and how our actions affect our lives and the lives of others.

A favorite definition of mine, from a book by Emmanuel Carerra, is "Meditation is anything you apply yourself to with love."

Love is free of self-interest, greed, jealousy, judgment and need for recognition.

Loving is not always easy to do. It takes practice.

Meditation practices tend to make loving easier.

Meditation, no matter how it is practiced, can open a door to the Inner World, to the Self.

And to an ultimate source of guidance.

Some call the ultimate source of guidance God, Jesus, Allah, Higher Power, Inner Witness or one of hundreds of names for a Supreme Being that come from various religious traditions.

I like to think of the ultimate source as Aliveness, the essence and energy of being alive.When we fill ourselves with Aliveness, through meditation or any other means, we naturally want to act in loving ways.

Ways that help heal the world.

YOUR TURN

It's time for me to stop. I think I've said enough.

Now, it's your turn!

ACKNOWLEDGEMENTS

Thank you to my loving and supportive family members, Sheila, Olivia and Kevin, Talia and Josh, Josh and Anna, Van, Izzy and Artie, Auggie, Tony and Betty, and to the family, friends and colleagues who read early drafts, encouraged me and provided thoughtful critiques. I am forever grateful to the memory of my mentor, Norman Bradford, Ph.D., who first showed me the way inside. And many thanks to the team at Luminare Press for expertly guiding my publishing journey!

To contact Reed Morrison,
email him at
reedamorrisonphd@gmail.com

Made in the USA
Middletown, DE
18 August 2023